SOCULITHERZ ON TV

The '20 FEISTY ENTERPRISE TIPS'

Interviews with Tony Robinson OBE

Copyright © The Business Advisory Bureau Limited

ISBN 978 1 8491488 18

Published by: BAB, The Business Advisory Bureau Limited, Publications January 2016

This book is licensed for your personal enjoyment only. It may not be sold or given away to other people. If you would like to share this book with another person, then please purchase an additional copy for each person. You may not reproduce this work, in part or in its entirety, without the express written permission of the author.

Most of the characters in this book and the co-author, Soculitherz, are fictitious. Any resemblance to real persons, living or dead is purely co-incidental.

Other books by Tony Robinson OBE with Soculitherz are

'**Buzzing with the Entrepreneurs**' Jan 2004 ISBN 0 9512488 39

'**Stripping for Freedom**' Jan 2010 ISBN 978 0 9512488 43

'**Freedom from Bosses Forever**' Aug 2014 ISBN 978 1 8491449 33

Allegedly, other books by Leonora Soculitherz are

'**The Edible Desire**' (1995);

'**Bong in the Orange Grove**' (1997);

Over Strung and Under Nourished (2002)

NEVER HAVE TO CROSS THE STREET TO AVOID SOMEONE

This was the advice that Tony Robinson OBE and Clare Francis were given by a business owner when they started their business in 1986. Integrity is a major asset to business owners but it has to be earned by living it. Helping each other as business owners, suppliers and customers is an important part of this. Tina Boden co-founded and co-funded with Tony the global, informal, free and indie Enterprise Rockers global movement on January 9th 2012.

On the second Friday of January #MicroBizMattersDay takes place where millions give a little time to help another. There is 8 hours live streaming of enterprise tips to help everyone keep going in their own business.

This special edition of 'Soculitherz on TV' was produced by Jo Harrison and Tony as a gift to the business owner guests and volunteers that give up their time to make the live streaming possible.'

SOCULITHERZ ON TV – 20 FEISTY ENTERPRISE TIPS

Is philanthropy a dirty word or just difficult to spell?

Hi, I'm Tony Robinson OBE. I'm not the famous comedy actor and television presenter. That's obvious, if I was I'd be in bed with a woman half my age, and twice as tall as me, and be doing other stuff rather than talking to you. I'm the one who looks like and has modelled himself on George Clooney and I am the UK agent for the Canadian fashionista, TV celebrity and investigative journalist, Leonora Soculitherz.

Soculitherz (pronounced So-cool-it-hurts) is now a single celebrity name like Rihanna (Ri-Ri), Madonna, Beyonce, Cher, Adele, Gaga and Batman. Soculitherz and I have collaborated for nearly ten years. Our most popular collaboration is the best-selling, and recently updated, book 'Freedom from Bosses Forever'. The whole idea of giving you this mini and cheap work of genius is that you'll change from being a cheapskate into a fabulous person who buys Freedom from Bosses Forever.

How was this TV series born?

Latterly, the mythical Soculitherz has been increasingly reclusive. So much so that drones were sent to her cave in the Yukon. Fortunately, a senior drone came back with the message that Soculitherz was willing to visit her 'least favourite country' because of the vast sums offered. Apparently, England is her 'least favourite country' because I live here.

The UK television broadcaster that commissioned the series of enterprise interviews with her had decided that I would be the ideal interviewer. They felt that the often spiky relationship we have – she thinks I'm an idiot – might make for good TV viewing.

Three of the, scheduled, six interviews were filmed. Then, quite mysteriously, the whole series was pulled. We suspect that the UK Government felt the interviews were 'off message' because Soculitherz refused to use the words 'entrepreneur', 'growth'. 'ambition', 'loan' and 'aspirational'. The official explanation was that Soculitherz had no credibility as a subject expert. Her jealous ex-husband, the cellist Gerard Brown, had posted a bollocks-naked selfie of him and Soculitherz, back in the day.

So the series was never aired but I managed to get hold of the recordings and transcribed the content into this mini book. I hope that you enjoy the brilliance of Soculitherz and that as a result you will want to buy 'Freedom from Bosses Forever'.

The Sense of Soculitherz

If you're thinking of being your own boss or are in the early months of going it alone then these Soculitherz interviews are for you. You're in for a real treat.

The idea for these interviews came to me during Global Entrepreneurship Week. Some TV celebrities, leading politicians and big company chief executives were speaking on what it takes to be a successful entrepreneur.

I was in an audience of thousands that were thinking of preparing to start or starting their own business. I realised that very little of what was being said would be relevant to the business they might start. I wasn't convinced that the speakers had gained their incomes from doing what they were asking the audience to do.

Those speaking on behalf of government initiatives, technology, communications and financial services companies just wanted to sell the concept of starting your own business for their own reasons. Worse still, I've been running my own business for 28 years and not a lot of the advice made sense to me.

The speakers were also trying to inspire the audience into building bigger businesses quicker than, in my opinion, was right or likely. I'm not against people thinking big but most of the multi-millionaire entrepreneurs I've met didn't have a big idea and didn't set out to be multi-millionaires. Most in the room did not possess the know-how or the kind of money, nor wanted to borrow the kind of money, that would have been required to achieve a 'big dream'.

After all, nine out of every ten new businesses are started by one, lone and brave, individual for whom investing all their money and time into their business is quite enough of a risk.

A friend and small business owner thought the presentations we were listening to were like a soufflé. They were light, sweet, airy, lively and cheerful. Indeed everyone could walk out the room feeling uplifted but the substance wasn't there to give the delegates a clear idea of what to do next to successfully start the business they wanted. That is, a business which would fit their aspirations, interests, skills, finances and personal circumstances.

Thankfully, the last speaker was my boss – Soculitherz (pronounced So-cool-it-hurts). Her full name is Leonora Soculitherz but a number of years ago she decided, like Madonna, Cher, Rihanna, Beyoncé, Gaga, Pele and Batman to go by a single celebrity name.

An intrepid investigator of how to go it alone

From the moment Soculitherz came on stage, until she ended her speech twenty minutes later, she made perfect sense to all the prospective business owners in the audience. Like the other speakers she is charismatic. She is also feisty, controversial, stunning, glamorous and very scary. She doesn't claim to be an entrepreneur or a business expert.

Soculitherz is, in her own words; 'a highly successful, super intelligent, classy, powerful business owner who wears the best designer clothes quite fabulously because I've got the kind of skinny, dream figure that makes most women want to poke my eyes out'.

Let me explain: Soculitherz is not only a television and radio celebrity she is a fashionista and lifestyle guru. In that respect she could be considered a highly successful freelancer. However, it is as a respected investigative journalist that she was given the opportunity to conduct hundreds of interviews, around the world, with small business owners and entrepreneurs.

Soculitherz explains what she has found are the most important, practical tips which will help everyone to start up, survive and thrive in their own business.

Soculitherz has received worldwide, critical acclaim from business owners and entrepreneurs that have become more successful, smarter, cooler and hotter as a result of her talks and books.

These talks often take place in her capacity as a Global Ambassador for the Enterprise Rockers and #MicroBizMattersDay Movement (http://EnterpriseRockers.com) which makes life better and fairer for micro business (0-9 employees) owners everywhere.

The published works

Soculitherz has collaborated with me on three bestselling books on Enterprise: Buzzing with the Entrepreneurs (2004), Stripping for Freedom (2010 – 2nd Edition) and Freedom from Bosses Forever (2013 and updated 2014).

She has also written hundreds of blogs and articles which include tips for business owners. Many of these blogs have been written for the No 1 Google ranked, The Small Business Blog (http://smeblog.com/author/leonorasoculitherz).

Her books, articles and blogs on enterprise include wide ranging investigations into government and corporate misuse of public funding for business support, employment and training. Some business gurus, politicians, academics, glampreneurs, bankers and government officials have been exposed by Soculitherz as 'shamsters, scamsters and snake oil peddlers'.

In these television interviews I've asked Soculitherz the important questions to elicit what those thinking of starting their own business will need to do in order to survive and thrive. This gives us the 'essential juices' of Soculitherz as it were. The Soculitherz juices which have so enthralled and excited her audiences around the world are all in this snug publication.

TV PROGRAMME ONE:

GETTING ENTERPRISE READY

Q. TR: Can everyone go it alone - be their own boss?

A. Soculitherz: Just how stupid are you, Mr. Tony Robinson OBE?

You've been in your own business for over thirty years without ever being successful. You are living proof that not everyone is cut out to start and run their own business.

Equally, many people, like you, have no alternative but to go it alone. This is not just because these people, like you, have no credibility as they've been spotted wearing a fleece. It's because they can't get a job or the job they could get doesn't suit their domestic circumstances. Anyway, most jobs and bosses suck.

Looking on the bright side, something I regularly have to do because I've got you as the worst agent in the world. If you can survive when your only skill is speaking gibberish, then most can.

One in seven of your country's workforce is self-employed and in most countries the number of self-employed is increasing annually. The majority of people will seriously consider self-employment at some stage in their working lives. Everyone can learn the skills to succeed – it is not difficult to learn these skills by doing.

It's a bit like looking good – wear stuff from great designers, look clean and tuck your bits in. It isn't difficult. It just requires common sense and bags of application. Persistence is the vital trait I've seen time after time in successful business owners.

You can start and run your own business, whatever your background, education or work experience. Probably, the less you've learned about corporate management or business theory the better. Starting your own enterprise is a fab career option for most people but it is not for everyone.

The majority that successfully start their own business don't do it expecting to become one of the world's greatest entrepreneurs but do it as a TINA (There Is No Alternative) or as a BOATEAL (Best Option Available To Earn A Living) or as an ERR (Escape the Rat Race – usually because they hate their boss or the politics).

The top reason for starting a business is about controlling one's own destiny not about making money. Most won't become fabulously wealthy, like me. In fact six out of ten will be earning less than the living wage, on an hourly basis, from their own business.

What that means is they tend to put in a lot of hours to make the income they need. The great thing though is that the vast majority are happy doing this.

So, usually it takes long hours and very hard work to make ends meet. Of the hundreds of business owners I've interviewed that have been successful, none have achieved it through a truly unique business idea.

They have all achieved success through persistence, hard work and learning by doing. It is worth it. Most people running their own business wouldn't swap it for an employed position.

TIP 1: SUCK IT AND SEE – FIND OUT IF THIS IS YOUR RIGHT TIME

If you have other ways of earning a living and, after reading this, you feel that you haven't enough know-how, or enough available time and money, to get through the first eighteen months of your own business – don't do it. Suck it and see whether there any customers that want your offer. It's best to do this whilst you're in a job.

In my opinion there is no better way to earn a living than being your own boss but ask other small business owners what it's like and whether they think you can do it.

Disgracefully, some of the people that are the most persuasive about 'everyone can start a business' or there's 'a business in you' or 'now is a great time to start' are people with fat salaries in jobs.

So, remember, you can always 'suck it and see' - do some business part time while in a full time or part time job. In some countries there are tax incentives to encourage this. Don't believe all that rubbish about needing to be full time in your business to be serious.

What you seriously need to know before you go full time is that you can get customers to buy your product or service.

Q. TR: You're the only person I've heard say that 'what's behind you is as important as what is in front of you'. I've no idea what you mean – please explain?

A. Soculitherz: Fortunately all my readers are significantly brighter than you, not difficult, but I will explain.

Whenever I've interviewed established and wealthy business owners as to why they succeeded, when many of the people that started at the same time as them didn't, they usually point to the people that helped them. The help takes many forms: money, advice, contacts, time, customers, motivation and resources. The person or people that helped them were there right from the start.

You may have spotted me at the Balenciaga fashion show in Paris last week. The front benches, which contain the A list celebs, collapsed. This meant we all had to stand for 'health and safety reasons'. This was good for me, as I was on the second row as an A minus celeb. It gave me a perfect view of the stick insects.

As I saw the startled VIPs, from the front row, collapsing onto their miniature bottoms or scrambling uncertainly to their feet, I thought about the snakes and ladders of both celebrity and running your own business.

Just as you think you've made it, to the best seats in the house, something can bring you down again in an instant. When we start our businesses it's all about avoiding the snakes who will offer us things we don't need, like premises, cars, insurances and consultancy. Then when we're finally established with a positive cash flow, it's all about avoiding the snakes that want a piece of our action, like buyers, suppliers, investors, partners, staff and the financial services sector - again.

These snakes not only sting they suck. They suck money and our most precious asset, and in very short supply, time, out of our business.

I'm just a successful, supercool, celebrity, fashionista that does a bit of investigative journalism about entrepreneurs on the side. But I do know the answer to how you can avoid these snakes?

From well before you start your business build your own support network of a few trusted friends and family. It's best if most of them have started and run their own business. They'll help you bootstrap rather than borrow from institutional or investor snakes. They'll help keep you fed and warm when there's little or no income. They'll understand and help you work the hours you need to work. They'll encourage you when nothing seems encouraging.

They'll still be behind you when your irreplaceable staff member blackmails you. They'll be there when the SEO/Social Media consultant wants your arm and leg and when the big company buyer wants a contract that would leave you with only one customer. They'll be there when the bank, or other snake after your money, rings you to offer you a new deal.

TIP 2: GET A SUPPORT NETWORK BEHIND YOU, SAY 'I'LL GET BACK TO YOU' AND THEN PHONE A FRIEND

Q. TR: Most countries have government schemes of free support for those thinking of starting a business. Why do you suggest going elsewhere for help?

A. Soculitherz: The scariest words to a prospective or existing small business owner are 'I'm from the government (or bank) and I'm here to help you'.

If the schemes and websites of free support for starting a business are primarily run and sponsored by government and financial services companies then B-E-W-A-R-E. My opinion is that they are often as much use as the 'Onesie' is to fashion (or for when you want to go to the toilet). Which reminds me I'll never forgive you for giving me one as a Christmas present – do I look like someone who has always yearned to be a zebra?

Some of this free advice is 'boiled down' big company business practice and much is produced by people that haven't successfully started their own self-employed or micro business. The advice is so yesterday. It is stuff from antiquity that belongs in a museum like you, my hopeless, ancient agent.

Most successful business owners I've interviewed operate in a very different but more dynamic, straightforward and flexible way than is recommended by government.

For a start, in the real world it is important to be constantly on the look-out for, and then taking, new opportunities to make money.

Much of what you do to grow your business is unplanned but your speed to exploit the opportunity and ability to make the deal – do some business – are vital.

TIP 3: DON'T PLAY BY THE RULES. THE RULE MAKERS ARE NOT PLAYING THE SAME GAME.

The downside of free start up advice from governments is that it is often their way of ensuring you comply with all their regulations and they collect the maximum amount of money from you.

Don't be an idiot and use all your time complying with red tape and regulations.

Most countries have so much bureaucracy and regulations in place to favour big business, and make it difficult for micro enterprise, that if you spent your time getting to understand all the regulations that could affect your business you'd be dead in the water before you'd started.

The irony is that, as you can see from the biggest financial services companies and energy companies they don't comply either. They gamble, often breaking the law on a massive scale and if they're found out they then settle out of court. It's how they make loads of money to pay themselves big salaries and bonuses.

You can't afford to do this because you can't afford the army of lawyers and accountants and settlement costs. You need to try to comply without wasting all your time in doing so.

If the successful business owners I've met had followed the advice on some of these government and bank backed business advice websites they wouldn't have built their businesses. For a start, most business owners I've met just copy stuff, like crazy.

Even the big swinging dicks in the entrepreneurship world like Trump, Sugar, Branson and Murdoch are copiers - with a twist - and deal makers. They didn't start out as the innovative, creative, hi tech pathfinders that governments suggest are the new businesses they want to support. Believe me there's a lot more people that won't make any money out of app development than do.

By the time most prospective business owners have done all the research and planning, that most government schemes recommend, they'd be too late in getting the product or service to market and the opportunity would have gone.

If they'd taken the government advice their money would be so tied up in supplier contracts (e.g. products, premises, energy, telecoms, financial services) or repayments to investors and lenders that not only would they have no cash to take advantage of deals to be made, but the slightest problem in their cash flow and they could be out of business.

Business is often about having a go at doing what someone else has tried before you. Look at Loubi (Christian Louboutin to you), if he hadn't read an article about a slashed out shoe with a red line, then thousands of rich women around the world wouldn't have fallen off his killer heels to, legs in the air, show off his signature red soles.

So, I'm not saying don't consider using your government's free start up support schemes as some are good but some are so bad they can actually cost you dearly.

By the way 'Start Up Canada', in my homeland, is not government run but run by volunteers and was founded by the inspirational, young social entrepreneur, Victoria Lennox. It is truly empowering. New Zealand's start up support programme is just excellent too – a really good combination of government working with private sector small businesses to help new small businesses.

TIP 4: SEEK ADVICE FROM THOSE THAT HAVE STARTED AND SUCCESSFULLY RUN THEIR OWN MICRO ENTERPRISE (0-9 EMPLOYEES)

Yes, I know that this means that there'll be some good advice that you'll ignore because it has come from someone that hasn't started a business. Equally, I'm not saying that you should accept all advice from those that have started and run a business. After all you, Tony Robinson OBE, are an example of someone that runs a business but whose advice I would never accept – mainly because I don't understand what you're saying. You can't even pronounce your own name properly.

I am saying that it is very, very dangerous to accept advice from those that haven't done something similar to what you want to do. It is usually safe to ignore all the stuff that looks like conventional business guidance.

I've done a quick Google and here are some of the topics which often are covered by 'conventional business guidance' and it is usually garbage: 'How to create a great business idea?', 'How to pitch your business idea to investors?', 'Getting finance' 'There's a business in you', 'Business planning', 'Get a mentor/coach' (often from a bank or corporate) and anything about technology or social media from a telecoms or technology or social media corporate.

Shock-Horror; Here's a tip that will upset you, my inept agent, Tony Robinson OBE, as you're from Yorkshire in England, a land where you expect everything for 'nowt' (free).

TIP 5: IT'S OFTEN BETTER TO PAY FOR PROFESSIONAL ADVICE THAN ACCEPT FREE ADVICE

Examples of free advice might be that provided or funded by national, regional or local government or banks or help from volunteer advisers, coaches and mentors that haven't successfully run their own businesses. It can be dangerous rubbish you get from them but because you're starting out you don't know that.

Most accountants and book-keepers have started and run their own business and offer a free initial consultation. If you're like me and you'd rather get out for a bit of retail therapy rather than you'll find messing around with numbers, tax collecting and form filling just too irksome. These boring bean counters can be useful bods.

Choose an accountant or book keeper, that's been in their own business for over three years. They'll help you to put together a realistic start up plan. Why? Because they'll have seen lots of their clients start up in the past and they can pass this knowledge onto you.

So, from what they've seen in the real world they'll be the best at estimating how much money you need and where you might get it, what are your realistic earnings, how to keep the cash flowing and how to minimise your costs – useful stuff huh?

Q. TR: I've heard you suggest to people new to running a business that they 'need to be in their enterprise zone' – what do you mean?

A. Soculitherz: Glad you've been listening – that must be a first.

Most successful entrepreneurs that I've interviewed haven't done any of the things that are regarded as 'good business practice'. The big business idea that most government and bank websites and academics talk about never came to them.

These entrepreneurs, like you and me, just decided to go into business – selling ourselves and any products and services we felt we could earn a living from selling.

Most of us don't like borrowing money, especially from banks – and worse, the Government (banks). Our business planning is in our heads or on a couple of pages of notes. Our brand is our personality. Most of us are action rather than words people. We copy and improve other people's ideas and activities like crazy.

The point is that time is money and opportunities come and go and we can't be wasting time on any theoretical 'business studies' type stuff. We don't have budgets because everything we spend has to give us a return.

If one road closes we look to go down another. If one idea or product bombs we test out others until we find a winner. What matters, the only thing that matters, is that we've decided to run our own enterprise and by hook or by crook, whatever hours it takes, we'll make it work – we'll make ends meet.

That's what I mean by being in your enterprise zone. Like winning the lottery you've got to be in it to win it.

TIP 6: FIND SOME BUSINESS OWNERS YOU CAN TRUST AND ASK THEM QUESTIONS

Then do something in return for these business owners so that you feel able to ask more questions another time. You help them to succeed and they'll help you to succeed. There is no better way. Collaboration is a fabulous way to grow a business. It is why the Enterprise Rockers and #MicroBizMattersDay Movement was founded (http://EnterpriseRockers.co.uk).

Existing micro enterprise owners know more about running a business than you do. Try out what they suggest. Some of it may not work but you'll only learn what works by doing, not by planning and thinking or trying to never make a mistake.

The Golden Soculitherz Rule, which has been adopted by the crazy #Enterprise Rockers @EnterpriseRocks, is: 'If you're starting and running a micro-biz (0-9 employees) only take advice from someone who has started and run a micro-biz or is employed by someone who has started and run a micro-biz'

Make your objective making money through your business not making your business idea work. Very few start-up business plans achieve the expected results. That doesn't matter if you're in your enterprise zone as it's all about adapting, changing, finding out what works and hanging in there but making money by as many means as you can.

When products or services aren't selling then test and try other products and services. It's obvious innit? Do this, get in your enterprise zone, and you've got an eight out of ten chance of surviving beyond three years – not bad odds eh?

TIP 7: LOOK FOR MULTIPLE INCOME STREAMS TO SURVIVE THE FIRST EIGHTEEN MONTHS

If you think of yourself as an enterprise zone rather than just one business type then it makes perfect sense to make enough money by whatever legal means to survive. This often means having many ways of earning money whilst your main business develops a customer base and a successful trading format.

You need as much help as you can get from family and friends to maximise the number of hours you can make money in each week. Then look for additional income streams. For example: online and offline trading opportunities (different product ranges if necessary); Sunday markets; fairs; trading globally; part time jobs; contract work; freelancing and so forth.

I know that I'm controversial in saying this but from what I've seen and experienced you stand a much better chance of hanging in there if you don't have 'all your eggs in one basket'. With so many online trading platforms, globally too, there is absolutely no reason why you should only have one income stream or business.

You can have products, services and customers in different sectors. You can have your own enterprise alongside distributorships and franchises. You can be employed and self-employed at the same time

Be prepared for one of these additional income streams to become your main income stream. It often happens that your first business, product or service doesn't work out as you expected but a better opportunity comes along or another product or service sells better. If you think of yourself as an enterprise zone then changing your main business, product or service is fine – you're prepared to be flexible.

The people that fail are the ones that over commit to their first business idea because they think it is a failure if it doesn't work. Being in business is the success – it doesn't matter which ideas, formats, products and services are the ones that work. Consider yourself an enterprise zone and go for multiple income streams – you'll learn a lot and it'll help you to make ends meet in the tough, first eighteen months.

TV PROGRAMME TWO:

KEEP GOING

Q. TR: A trait you've observed in successful start-ups is what you call 'an enterprise mind set'. What is this and how does one get it?

A. Soculitherz: On the day you start trading you are on your own and vulnerable - you are your business and your brand.

Friends and colleagues may stand back to see whether you succeed or not. They may even disappear in case you ask them to help you. Worse, your friends that have never started their own business suddenly become expert at it. If you're young – you're 'too inexperienced' to succeed' and if you're old, like you Tony Robinson OBE, then it's 'too late' – you're past your sell by date.

It's never too early or too late, if you go into it in a wholehearted, sensible way and are willing to listen to people that are running their own business. As I said in 'Stripping for Freedom' you may have to divest yourself of these 'friends', jerks, for a while so that you can focus on proving them wrong.

Previous employers may not answer your call. Most of the calls you get will be people trying to sell you stuff. Your first customers may take advantage of you – usually on credit – that is they don't pay you for ages.

Your first suppliers will give you no credit and may inflate the price to you as a newbie. Having an enterprise mind set helps you get through these early days.

As a Canadian I may for just a millisecond put up with being mistaken for an American, but I won't tolerate what I call 'chumminess'. Only my friends and family and perhaps my celebrity stalker, who e-mails me the sweetest things, are allowed to tease me about the lengths I'll go to enhance my public persona.

If highlights, extensions, affairs or even icing my nipples makes me stand out from the crowd, then it is not only my business, it is only me doing business. This is me with my enterprise mind-set in my enterprise zone.

TIP 8: THERE'S NO ROOM FOR WEENIES IN THE GLOBAL ENTERPRISE COMMUNITY – JUST GET ON WITH IT

If I was employed in a corporate then I'd be stuck in a rut. I'd have to wait for permission. I'd have to follow branding guidelines. I'd have to remain on plan. I'd rely on formal contracts rather than my ability to negotiate – make a deal. I'd have normal work hours, normal delivery hours, normal trading terms – 'normal' is not enterprising.

I know you, Tony Robinson OBE, have a crush on the Williams sisters so let me use an example from Serena to explain the mind set you need to succeed.

The Williams sisters have raised the game, opportunity and fashion in women's tennis but they are most definitely not who the tennis establishment expected to be their sport's trailblazers.

As you, my hapless and hopeless agent are not, by any means, the sharpest knife in the drawer, you don't realise that what the Williams family achieve provides some great learning for micro business owners the world over. It also captures a lot of what that fab Enterprise Rockers and #MicroBizMattersDay movement is about.

Last year, there was a lot of controversy at the Madrid Open about the new blue coloured clay courts. They use blue playing surfaces indoors in tennis and in other sports, like hockey, as it make the game better for spectators and television.

However, the men, particularly the world's number 1 and 3 at the time, Djokovic (cool) and Nadal (hot), didn't like these blue, normally red, clay courts. They said it was too slippery. They threatened to boycott any future tournaments that used it.

This is what Serena Williams had to say, in her winner's interview, about the playing surface:

"Women are way tougher than men," she said. "That's why we have the babies; you guys could never handle kids….. We ladies don't complain we just do our best. On the WTA we are real performers, we are not about going out there and being weenies."

Go Serena go. Now neither Serena nor I have had babies but I think you can see what she's getting at. By the way, I wonder if she hasn't had babies for the same reasons I haven't. I'm just not convinced that the maternity or new Mum look is for me – why I've even seen some of these women go outside without their mascara on!

The point is there's really no point in whining - just get on with it. I believe women are better at just getting on with it. Look at Tina Boden, for example, co-founder of the global Enterprise Rockers and #MicroBizMattersDay global community. Follow her on twitter – be inspired.

TIP 9: TO BE PERSISTENT ENOUGH TO SUCCEED YOU HAVE TO LOVE BEING IN YOUR OWN BUSINESS

All the successful micro business owners, women and men, I've interviewed work longer and harder and against greater odds than their corporate and public sector equivalents. Yet, because they love being in their own business they remain incredibly positive. That is an enterprise mind set.

Q. TR: When I was a young lad my parents had their own business and I hated everything about business and especially selling. If you haven't any natural abilities for business can you still learn how to start up and succeed?

A. Soculitherz: Funny thing is I've always thought of you as ancient, and certainly from another planet, but I suppose you must have been young once – were you born with a beard?

The big difference between business as taught in colleges and universities and business as run by real, live, business owners is 'guts and passion'. If you don't have the enterprise know-how when you start your business the good news is that if you've got the guts and passion to hang in there you'll learn what you need to know and do for your business very quickly.

Let me tell you about my background. I lived my early years in Hull, close to Ottawa, in Canada. My house was called 'The Parsonage'. It was up a steep road, separated from the other houses, and it overlooked a grim churchyard. In truth, it was a greyish place, surrounded by bleak, undulating moorland, with just eight bare rooms and a stone staircase.

I was one of three sisters and I had an older brother who I regarded as something of a genius. Many people thought we were talented. We created light, colour, beauty and a fantasy world out of sand, water, blu-tack, paper clips and sweet wrappers. We weren't allowed glue because of my brother Grayson's tendency to sniff it.

We would each take a side of the sand pit, with me, Leonora, (as a child I wasn't the single celebrity name I now am) directly opposite Grayson. The sandpit would represent far off and foreign lands populated by little colourful people whom we'd make out of the paperclips, blu-tack and sweet wrappers. This is probably where I first gained an eye for fashion.

I would be Queen Antonia, The Reasonable. Grayson would be King George, The Junior. Together we ruled the kingdom of Gundoil, where all the Gundoilers did as we said. The mission of us, the Gundoil rulers, was to effect regime change in other lands. Basically we blew them up, so that we could make huge amounts of money selling construction, arms, drugs and fast food franchises to these other lands whilst taking all their natural reserves of energy back to Gundoil.

I learned the first big rule of enterprise which is 'when you get money and power buy other people's businesses and properties - it's a lot quicker way to grow than building customers for your business'

My sisters were the opponents of Grayson and me. They were the Grand Protectors of the Funny Foreign Lands and they had to avoid provoking Gundoil, Grayson and I, into attacking and annexing their lands. The fantasy was played out in silence, so that the other side couldn't hear the other side's plans or suspect their duplicity.

We communicated in tiny writing, often in heroic verse, on sweet wrappers which we then made into little airplanes which we flew across the sandpit to our partner in crime.

We had thought about publishing the contents of all these sweet wrappers to show off our brilliance to the world, but unfortunately Grayson had a nasty streak which combined with his glue sniffing habit made him not the ideal co-author, co-ruler and business partner. When Grayson took a dislike to anything he didn't understand he would just throw a bucket of water over everything in the sand pit.

Eventually, we three sisters got fed up with rebuilding our world and we were also getting really fat from eating all the sweets.

Now, you could think that this enterprising background, as a child, is the reason for my fabulous success. The main reason, of course, for my success is that I turned what I loved doing, my passion, into earning a living. I just loved fashion and looking and being better than everyone else. However, the games we played gave me useful skills with numbers, with communicating, selling my ideas, with showing off, with problem solving and so forth.

There's a fabulous book, by an Enterprise Rocker, Lorraine Allman with Mary Cummings, called 'Enterprising Child'. It shows parents how they can give their children, through play, these vital life skills. With luck this will ensure future generations aren't miserable moaners, like you, that grew up hating everything to do with business.

But, I'm glad you recognise that selling is a vital skill.

TIP 10: DITCH THE BUSINESS PLAN – FIND A CUSTOMER TO SELL TO

Whatever the product or service you are thinking of offering, you must test and practice selling it to prospective customers. You might need to change the product or service offer if you find it too difficult to sell.

Don't let the experts lull you into believing 'business planning is the most important skill'. Of course you need to have a clear idea of where you're going and how you're going to get there and the numbers attached to this but 'winning and keeping customers' through your own efforts, is the 'must have' skill.

Winning more business (through selling) and looking after customers are what 99% of new business owners need to get great at pronto. No customers equals no business.

You, Tony Robinson OBE are a prime example of someone who wastes hours each day promoting my talents, as a speaker and author, on Twitter and other social media but at the end of the day you haven't made a single sale. Why is that oh useless one? Because you haven't been selling or negotiating with a prospective customer.

Because you are passionate about your products and/or services you will find a method of selling and win-win negotiating that you find comfortable with – if you practice. It's usually about asking really, helpful to the customer, questions so that you can provide them with what they want.

Before you start trading most business owners would recommend you test out your products and/or services with potential customer. Not only are you testing whether you've got your product or service right – you're also learning how to sell it.

For products; car boot sales and markets can be ideal testing grounds and for business to business services then exhibition stands (share one) and business fairs are great. Skype and free webinars are other ways to test trade (sell).

Q. TR: Where's the best place to get the money to start up?

A. Soculitherz: OMG. For crying out loud 'what is the point?' Aaaaargh = look what you've done - driven me to eat another family size carton of chocolate brownies.

The Soculitherz global enterprise is suffering from a distinct lack of motivation, not helped by having you, Tony Robinson OBE – the agent from hell – losing me more business than you'll ever bring in because you don't listen to a word I'm saying. Is there a care home for hapless and hopeless agents that we can put you in?

I remember when I first met you. I'd anticipated being introduced to a famous comedy actor and television presenter. Instead, this talentless, fashion disaster appeared in front of me.

You tripped over your briefcase, threw your red wine over my Stella McCartney, introduced yourself as 'Yarm Turnie Robbins' and continued to mispronounce most of the English language whilst clumsily mopping me and my dress with your tie.

I should have sued you rather than work with you. The correct question is: 'How do I make ends meet when starting my own business?' Your question is not helpful to the enterprise mind-set which I want my readers and devoted fans to adopt.

One thing you did get right was befriending and learning from the soooo cool Tim Campbell MBE, the first TV 'The Apprentice' Winner in the UK. You also learned from his boss who was your client many years ago, Lord Sugar - the Donald Trump equivalent - host of 'The Apprentice' in the USA. Surprisingly, for me anyway, you wrote a good article about what you'd learned from Campbell and Sugar. I quote from it, from time to time. You wrote:

'I love Lord Sugar's tale, hope I get this right, that in the early days of his business he'd try to sell all he needed to by Wednesday to cover all the week's costs so that all the margin from sales on a Thursday and Friday went straight to assets.'

This is the right attitude that I've seen proven by business owners the world over. It says I'll make the money to invest in my business – rather than where can I borrow the money to build a business.

I know this may go against everything my readers will have seen before about starting a business. But I am Soculitherz and these other writers are not.

TIP 11: BOOTSTRAP DON'T BORROW

Sure, there will be exceptions. If you come up with a brilliant new invention that you're going to manufacture there may be no alternative but to borrow to make the prototype, to protect the intellectual property and so forth. Even then, if you can get the money through your own means or with your family and friends it is usually better than borrowing from a bank or an investor.

In my opinion from everything I've investigated, when most people ask the question 'Where can I get the money to start a business', they're looking for a loan to tide them over with their personal and business expenses until they start making money.

With a formal loan from an institution or an investor, the new business owner loses vital control of the business. The plug can be pulled by the lender or they start interfering in your business – it's like having a boss again – it sucks.

Bootstrapping, which I do recommend, means pulling yourself up over the business hurdles in front of you, by your own bootstraps.

So what kind of things would you do as a bootstrapper? You make some money to invest in your business. You borrow short term from friends and family. You might do credit terms deals with suppliers, you might do deals with customers to get some payments up front, some interim payments, perhaps, even a bonus on delivery or for outstanding service.

You get free help to build your business from your network, you work from home, you use the cloud, you use 'cheap as chips' (a Brit expression) apps and open source software, you earn from a job as well, you do deals to raise money and you sell your CD/DVD/Books/Jewellery/Antiques/Batman/Clothes (not shoes) collections. You may even sell your car or house or get a repayment holiday on both.

You trade on e-bay, Amazon and Etsy, you become a film extra and you sell your sperm (probably more applicable to men). You barter and you get free, volunteer help from friends and family (repay them when you do get money) Do you get the idea? Make money to invest in the products and services that you can trade to get more money to invest in your business.

Do it yourself and be in control. It may seem slower but trust me it is better. The big risks in business come from owing an investor or an institution before you've even learned how to succeed in your own business.

Down the way, once you're a proven success and have assets for lenders to secure loans against, you can have your loan. Never get a loan to cover your salary. Business doesn't work like that.

I should come clean with you about one naughty, risky, little bootstrapping trick many of us business owners have done in desperation. You must realise that I've been more desperate than most having Tony Robinson OBE as my agent.

The naughty trick is that we've used our personal credit cards to either buy stuff to sell or cover some of our personal and business expenses whilst we're waiting for customer payments. What am I like?

As long as we can repay most of it within the month we get away with this naughty trick as a last resort. Never, ever max out the credit cards unless you know the sales and profit to come will allow you to pay it all off pronto. So, natch, I'm not advising you do this but, hey, it's bootstrapping too.

Q. TR: Your book before your 'tour de force' and 'best-selling' and 'must buy', 'Freedom from Bosses Forever' was called 'Stripping for Freedom'. For those that haven't read it – can you explain why you believe 'stripping' is important in order to survive the early months and years as your own boss?

A. Soculitherz: That's a pretty cool question. As, in theory, you are my agent you could have said; 'the hugely popular, funny, priceless, award winning 'Stripping for Freedom, now improved and updated as 'Freedom from Bosses Forever' but, as usual, you blew it.

Firstly I really applaud all who have a go at starting and running their own enterprises. They're making something out of nothing and that's a great achievement. As I've already said, most don't borrow and don't want investor partners - they want to control their own destiny – do it for themselves.

From all the self-employed and successful business owners I've interviewed I'm convinced that those that succeed need to be incredibly focused and hard working in their business, particularly in the first, vulnerable, 18 months.

This requires 'Stripping for Freedom'. It means divesting yourself of everyone and everything that will get in the way of you controlling your own enterprising destiny.

I'm sure that this might sound incredibly selfish but I'm just calling it as I see it, from having interviewed many hundreds of small business owners plus many famous entrepreneurs. You'll be able to repay your family and friends for helping you through the vulnerable early months and years but you do need to strip for freedom.

Many successful entrepreneurs do much for free to build a positive reputation and get themselves into networks that contain money and influence. The big 'I am' doesn't work when you're starting out.

TIP 12: GET INTO NETWORKS THAT GIVE YOU KNOW-HOW AND FUN

Choose carefully with your business networks. Informal networks may be best. Most business networking meetings are an absolute waste of time. It doesn't matter whether they are online or offline, time is the one resource you cannot afford to waste. Many networks seem like a lot of desperate people hoping for a break in the clouds and a bagful of money to descend on them.

So, choose networks that include people that you can give happiness and know how to because there's a good chance they can give happiness and know how to you too. Never be afraid to build trust in your products and services by giving something for free. Networks are great if they are reciprocal.

All successful entrepreneurs whom I've met have had to work bloody hard and remain focused on creating opportunities for them and their business. They've all had to make sacrifices to succeed.

They are also enterprising (go into situations others would regard as risky) and brilliant self-promoters. They are frank, forthright and have an unshakeable sense of what is right. They are highly 'professional' (meet every commitment), self-sufficient and totally believe they can make their own luck. They are the kind of positive people that others like to be around.

Most of them take great pride in their personal appearance – looking good. I'm not talking Hollywood here. Have a look at all the athletes in the Paralympics again. They all looked absolutely fabulous – hot even. They care and put in the hard yards and we admired them for it. They were supreme ambassadors for their sport because of the level they achieve. You need to be the supreme ambassador for your business.

Looking good today isn't a statement that 'I've got good genes'; it's saying 'that's what I choose to spend some of my time and money on'. It is your choice. No right and no wrong. If you want to do it, then do it.

If you're thinking that this all sounds a bit improbable, scary even, and doesn't sound like you – don't worry – most successful entrepreneurs weren't like this right at the beginning. But they soon got themselves, through willpower, heading in the right direction.

Selflessness, focus, productivity and belief are the positive traits that I would have you copy.

From my interviews with successful business owners it is clear that the separation of business and personal lives is to be recommended for everyone. Your business persona has to be harder, than how you are with the people you trust and love in your domestic life, to cope with rejection and people taking advantage of you. Your business persona must remain focused on the here and now.

Women are often more willing to take advice and training to achieve the aims on which they're focused and will carefully build a trusted support network. They are very productive and meet the business needs during their working hours. So if you're a man going it alone – follow a woman. If you're a woman – don't follow a man.

This belief transmits itself to new and existing customers, which makes business building through credible selling and high quality of supply much easier.

By the time I'm finished with you you'll be enterprise ready, fashionable, life knowledgeable and primed for success like a cocked trigger.

You're also ready to be naked now. Actually, although I love clothes, I always prefer to be naked because clothes make me feel fatter. If you're ready to go into business for yourself, then you're ready to be exposed.

You are exposed because whatever status and profile you had when you were employed is stripped away. Your former colleagues and associates will disappear, as they'll be worried you may fail or, worse, you may ask them to do something to help you.

Confidence is vital in making your business a success by selling your products and services. You get this confidence by testing out your business idea and feeling good about your mind and body.

TIP 13: KICK ASS BEFORE YOU START – TONE UP YOUR MIND, BODY AND BUSINESS IDEA

Your mind and business idea you'll strengthen by getting feed-back from potential customers and people that have got the T shirt from reading this book and doing what you're going to do.. There are many ways to get your body right and I won't turn this into one of my fabulous books on nutrition, like the Choco-Wine diet, which I swear by. I'd rather you bought those books to make me more money. But I will just give you my take on exercise.

Treat your body mean. Forget about treadmills, bikes, steppers and rowing machines. Go straight for the weights. Apart from my Marlborough Light habit, laxatives and occasional finger down the throat, I put my sleek figure down to a great diet and joining a proper gym.

I mean the kind of gym where they sweat, sniff salts, men scratch balls, women kick ass, curse, yell, groan and the weights smash down on the concrete as they let them go. The kind where you only wear black and you open your Lucozade Sport drink when no-one's looking in case it takes you more than one go to flip the top.

When you've used all of these 20 Tips you'll be so confident that you'll be like a guru. What is a guru like? Well they're paid the big bucks for stating the obvious. That the obvious is so interesting to others is because it works. You'll feel you know better than anyone else, because it's your business, what works for you and your business and you'll feel confident that you're the person to put it all into action.

TV PROGRAMME THREE:

CUTTING THROUGH THE NOISE

Q. TR: I can tell you loved the Paralympics. When you were at the London Olympics you said that there were lessons to be learned for people about to start out in business. Did you mean; how to be gorgeous like Jessica Ennis?

A. Soculitherz: You're a disgrace Robinson. Jessica Ennis is a superb example of having a clear vision of what success looked like in each of her events, a plan to get to each vision and the ability and attitude to execute the plan.

Above all an elite athlete has to put in days, months and years of dedicated practice so that they can execute their plan and achieve that vision. They don't just start off as a world beating athlete. From talking to business owners, it's the same about starting a business. If you hang in there with your start up, then the longer you run your own business the better you'll get at it. That's why bootstrapping to survive the first, vulnerable eighteen months of your business is so important.

Stella McCartney, who designed the Team GB Olympics kit, said 'You don't need to sacrifice style for sport'. Stella clearly wasn't aware that you, my hapless, hopeless, fashion disaster of an agent, Tony Robinson OBE, was going to attend two weeks of the Olympics.

I blame your London Mayor, Boris Johnson. He had the security and the opportunity to stop you, my imbecile of an agent. But, despite my warnings, he let you in. One sad Yorkshireman, and I do know that if Yorkshire was a nation it would have been twelfth in the medals table, lowered the tone of the greatest show on earth for billions.

Actually, I thought that fashion won few medals at the Olympics. Stella's stuff was better than Giorgio's Italy get up and Ralph's US rags but the best was Cedelia Marley's, daughter of Bob, Jamaican kit. I thought that the yellow and green of Jamaica rocks and what's not to like about Messrs. Bolt and Blake.

I tried to give, my new best friends – Usain and Yohan – an autographed copy of my best seller 'Stripping for Freedom' after they won the relay but some Brit with a machine gun stopped me. Don't they know who I am?

Later, in the Olympics, you may have seen me jump into the pool with Tom Daley and his entourage after he won his bronze. Can't think why but I did enjoy the men's, body hair free zone, diving and swimming a lot.

It was a wonderful two weeks at the Olympics, except when I spotted you, Robinson throwing your red wine (£5.20 a go) and food over innocent spectators.

I digress, yes I did learn a lot about how small business owners can win against the bland big corporates who had the Olympics stitched up between them.

As in 'Proud to accept only Visa'

Visa, Coca Cola, McDonalds, (why do these companies get funded by your Brit government to do their staff training etc.?) and the rest of the Olympics' sponsors have done well because the millions of visitors to Olympic venues could only buy their products or use their services. However, they did themselves no favours at all in becoming trusted and liked by customers and consumers.

I'm certain that the sheer blandness, corporateness, creativeless, sameness and valueless of their offer at the hugely successful London 2012 will prove a good thing for small and micro business. Most consumers given the choice will prefer to buy from independent, owner-led micro enterprises.

Here are four tips, from my Olympic experience, to incorporate into your new business. These tips build on the anti-corporate/government feeling that prevails amongst the majority of consumers.

TIP 14: MAKE DEALS TO PROSPER

Be flexible – there's nothing like a win-win on price and product/service offer to make both the customer and the biz owner friends for life. Every minute you enter into conversation with your customers builds a relationship and allows you to negotiate a deal that meet their needs exactly.

The corporates and government bodies only offer 'identical' and 'take it or leave it'. No wonder their employees looked fed up whilst all the volunteer games makers, using their own initiative, looked so happy.

Ensure everyone you employ or you contract or partner with has the same ability to make a deal on your behalf. Customers prefer doing things there and then – when they're hot they're hot. I know I'm hot and immaculate all the time but not all of your customers will be. So ensure the deal can be done there and then by whoever is in front of the customer.

TIP 15: BE DIFFERENT – NO SHEEP DIPS HERE

In my hundreds of interviews with enterprise owners one of the mistakes, many have admitted to, was in trying to mimic the corporates rather than differentiate from them. The Olympics was saved from feeling like one giant sheep dip from your government and the big global corporates by the sheer energy, laughter, tears and diversity of the spectators, the volunteers and the athletes.

Be creative. There are, at least, twenty ways an independent cafe owner can attract people to their cafe rather than Starbucks or McDonalds. A micro baker, confectioner, florist, butcher, pharmacy, electronic retailer can find another twenty ways to attract customers to their premises rather than Tesco or Wal-Mart. Even a 'work from home' accountant can find enough ways for their fee paid start up support to be taken up rather than a government or charity's free equivalent.

Ensure your business has something for everyone. Embracing diversity is really tough for 'the suits' as was proven at the Olympics yet it's the easiest thing in the world if you're interested in finding out about people. Everyone is an individual and every micro enterprise owner can add value in different ways to every potential and existing customer. It only requires questioning and listening.

TIP 16: PUT PASSION AND FUN INTO YOUR BUSINESS - PRICELESS

The Olympics was a triumph for the athletes, the volunteers and the spectators because they and their emotions were authentic. It contrasted starkly with all the 'spin' around the games organisation and sponsorship.

Customers and consumers are smart and quick. Quick because the technology to spread the word that people love you, or don't, is almost instantaneous. If you want your business to be loved by your customers you need to love your business and your customers. Change your business if you don't.

At the end of the events and at the closing ceremony the smiles on the faces of the athletes were priceless. Those smiles are worth millions too in them selling themselves because it's natural – the fun and the passion is authentic. Mo Farah, double gold winner, epitomised this fun and passion and put all of his success down to 'hard graft'

If you're going to succeed in your own business then you'll need to work long and hard. You might as well enjoy it too. Choose a business that matches your passion and gives you fun – the customers will love it.

You need to fuel your passion and fun in order for it to keep burning in your biz, like the Olympic torch. That means surrounding yourself with people you enjoy being with that are positive about what they do too. Why do you think I spend 99% of my time with the Stellas, Ralphs. Giorgios, Yohans, Usains, Tinas and Clares of this world and close to zilch with Tony Robinson OBE?

Finding the time to spend with Usain and Yohan hasn't been easy, I can tell you. I've been smack up against a publisher's deadline. I've been finishing off my latest erotic thriller, '50 Sheds du Lait'. It's about a fit French dairy farmer investigating the disappearance of big supermarket bosses. Anyway, writing the 'ooh la la' first meeting of the stylish lady chief of police with the farmer with the fabulous six pack, reminded me how unfortunate I'd been to ever meet you, Tony Robinson OBE.

TIP 17: CASHFLOW IS QUEEN – GET YOUR CLAWS OUT FOR CASH

There is something you've said to me, Robinson, over the years that has proven true for successfully starting and running your own business. You said 'Focun widding cussmers ankajfleur iskin' which translated means 'Focus on winning customers and cash-flow is king'.

Even I, a celebrity fashionista, best-selling author and investigative journalist, can sometimes get distracted by such as tall, lean but muscled athletes at the Olympics or Brad Pitt. One can forget to focus on winning customers and that cash flow is king but one does so at one's peril.

Customers and cash flow do come together every time I negotiate a new client contract. Fight hard, tooth and nail, to get cash into your business as quick as you can. Cash is the lifeblood of your business. You cannot grow a business without a positive cash-flow.

For example, I've realised negotiating what the client sees as a lower daily rate for my services in exchange for an annual contract is a fantastic deal. This gives me monthly payments directly credited to my account on the first of each month.

Similarly, if I'm working in a country where I need office premises for me and my team of hunks, then I'd rather pay a little more for easy in, easy out terms – I can get out with a week or a month's notice rather than get tied into a fixed term lease.

Naturally, negotiating credit terms with your suppliers is a must too. The longer you can delay the better. But do not fall into the trap many start-ups do of accepting a deal that looks fantastic with good payment terms but which actually ties up your cash. So, you don't need a year's supply of business stationery or a 3 year maintenance agreement on all your technology or an effing pension scheme when you start up. Pay all your suppliers within thirty days – it is only fair.

I had a friend starting up that thought contracting with a magazine for a year's advertising paid quarterly was fantastic. What an idiot – he'd committed all the money he had for marketing into advertising that he hadn't proved worked just because it looked a good deal. If in doubt, spend little and often and keep the cash moving.

When you've negotiated the best deal you can on payment terms with your customers and clients you've still got get cute and fight to get your bill paid on time. You may even like to offer a discount for early payment when you submit your invoice. Make this big, black and bold on the invoice.

Before you submit your first bill, find out the name of the person that will be processing your bill. Seven to ten days before your bill is due to be paid phone them to check everything is OK and you will be paid on time. You'll probably find your bill has been 'lost in the system' so you'll need to ring daily until it is found. If your client doesn't pay on time then make it clear on your reminder statement that legal action is automatic after a certain number of days.

Don't worry about losing the client. If they're in the habit of trying to get away with the late payment then then they are likely to respond first to those suppliers that are serious about taking them to court. Anyway, there are some clients; frankly, you just can't afford to have - if they delay your payments too long. Start-ups are very vulnerable to big companies and government agencies taking advantage of them with impossibly long payment terms.

I've recommended that all Governments should take the lead in their countries It's pitiful that Banks and the Big Supermarkets pay their bills in over 60 days. They call that prompt payment – instant death to micro enterprises, more like.

Government should ensure that national, regional and local government, all their agencies, all their suppliers and all organisations they provide public funding to support, should pay their bills within 30 days. They haven't done it yet so get ready to kick ass.

Q. TR: I've got nearly 13000 followers on Twitter @TonyRobinsonOBE and @EnterpriseRocks has the same does that make me a social media success?

A. Soculitherz: The only thing you've been successful at is murdering the English language.

Let me explain. Your website http://TonyRobinsonOBE.com works OK in describing what you offer a client but are you using social media effectively to generate the maximum amount of interest and leads to you and your products and services? Anyone starting a business today must learn how to use social media as a part of their marketing and promotion. But people like you are vulnerable, I might say, pathetic, souls.

Because you've never had any friends, for obvious reasons, then having lots of followers and Facebook 'likes' is exciting for you - but it may not mean a thing in gaining business. You waste most of your day talking to a blank, virtual wall.

Social media activity comes with a wealth warning – don't put all your marketing and promotion time into it. Twitter, Facebook, LinkedIn, Pinterest, Instagram, Google+ are the main ones I use and I'm pretty sure you can get another couple of years out of all of these.

Of all these I've had more leads from Twitter but equally I know many product suppliers that swear by Facebook and service providers that swear by LinkedIn.

The important thing is that dismal word 'engagement'. Broadcasting is rubbish – you need to meet people in social media. So let's take Twitter as an example. You have 140 characters to use. Use them to create a conversation with others. Key hours for Twitter are 8 – 10am, 11 – 2pm, and 6 -9pm, remember to engage and be engaging, and do re-tweet others if they are relevant to your business. Don't just tweet … "We make cupcakes that look like penises' - you simply won't engage with others!

Many people say that websites are not as important as your activity in social media but I believe they are complementary. Using social media to drive people to ask for a price or to buy from your website is as proven a promotional tactic as was a direct mailer to a target audience to ask them to telephone a help line.

Decide if you are likely to retail online, of if your website is for information or reassurance to your market. Do include details of what you make, who you are and where people will be able to buy your products or services from.

Do remember to include your name and business address as well. Government and Corporates don't give a damn about customers which is why their executives are at the top of the ivory tower and nowhere near the point of sale. That's where you as a micro enterprise owner have a winning advantage. Make sure your website and all your social media profiles make it clear how they can get to talk to you - a real, and interested in the customer, person!

TIP 18: YOU CAN EASILY BEAT CORPORATE ON SOCIAL MEDIA AS A PERSON – YOU ARE YOUR BRAND

Q. TR: I really like your red leather boots. You write blogs and appear on many sites, like Pinterest, with your choco-wine diet but doesn't doing all this free stuff get in the way of earning a living from your own business?

A. Soculitherz: How many times have I told you – your passion for your products and services plus integrity, in all you do, makes your USP? I want the world to be slim, funky, happy, fulfilled, fit, and, just a tad, squiffy, on my choco-wine diet.

My 'choco-wine diet' board and 'men's fashion faux pas' boards are amazingly popular on Pinterest. My blogs on the Small Business Blog are some of the most read on the web. Why? Because what I write makes sense. Anything that makes sense is freely available – just ask someone that's been there and got the T shirt. I can't charge people for what is obvious – 'drink red wine daily and eat dark chocolate to feel fab' – but they know I'm authentic and so will buy my other stuff.

Unfortunately, what works in business isn't as obvious as dark chocolate and red wine. Corporate and institutional management, like Government, are lost in a parallel world of applying management techniques, jargon, planning, processes, meetings, presentations, reports and handling internal politics. It is easy for a small business owner or freelancer to tell massive corporations of highly qualified managers what to do - because what they're doing is bollocks. There are a small number of multi-millionaires who have never worked in a large corporation coaching large corporations on management and leadership – hands up, I'm one.

So how does that work then? One of the reasons for the continuing global meltdown of big companies and major institutions is because their directors and managers are just not as entrepreneurial as small business owners. They are rule and precedent bound, rather than breaking new ground. They wait for marketing to work rather than go out selling. They have to make high risk deals, knowing prosecution and settlement may follow, they fiddle the books or go for dodgy investments in order to survive, as they can't grow by providing stuff that people want and will pay for.

They could be interested in customers but they're not really bothered because earnings are now the holy grail. In truth, the more senior they are the less they can do. If they want anything doing they hire a consultant. Often their internal culture has led to them not understanding the real world anymore, so they cannot have the same bias for useful action as someone starting or running their own enterprise.

TIP 19: THERE IS NOWT (A ROBINSON PHRASE MEANING 'NOTHING') USEFUL YOU CAN LEARN ON STARTING AND GROWING A BUSINESS FROM HIGHLY QUALIFIED, COPORATE MANAGERS AND LEADERS

This tip 19, is probably obvious but I make it because there are many people in jobs, with salaries, that believe they know more about starting and running a business than those that have started and run a business. It is weird but true – don't listen to them.

AT THIS POINT IN THE TELEVISION PROGRAMME SOCULITHERZ, WITH A FLAMBOYANT GESTURE, POINTED TO A SCREEN BEHIND HER AND SAID:

Let's take one successful entrepreneur, Stefan Topfer, Editor of the Small Business Blog and Chair/Owner of WinWeb and one unsuccessful one, you (pointing at me), Tony Robinson OBE. They have two things in common; they're both badly dressed (fleeces – urgh) but they look for business opportunities all the time.

So, yesterday, I recorded Robinson ringing Topfer. Here is their conversation:

Robinson: I've just seen on the BBC News site that a scientist has proven that giant dinosaurs could have warmed the earth with their flatulence.

Topfer: Ja – I mean, so?

Robinson: Well, where is the equivalent place today where hundreds of dinosaurs, produce masses of hot air?

Topfer: In your House of Commons and House of Lords?

Robinson: Precisely and why will this supply of huge volumes of hot air continue ad infinitum?

Topfer: Would that be because it is mainly a boys club eating vast quantities of posh nosh provided by the City and the top 100 CEOs and one or two media moguls?

Robinson: Yeah, that, and their humongous expense accounts that they can spend on Big Macs and pasties. It makes you feel good to know that we can now recycle all that dinosaur fuel for the benefit of the people.

Topfer: Ja, I mean nein, I mean how?

Robinson: You're fab at technology, do the math and turn Parliament into a massive great hot air heater which channels warmth into the council housing, parks, stations and doorways where those with no dosh to pay for heating live.

I won't carry on – as Topfer told you never to speak to him again. The point is that here were two dinosaurs discussing a business opportunity from a source of natural energy that has been available for thousands of years.

There's nothing original here apart from the possible opportunity.

You, Robinson, are an idiot but Topfer is a millionaire entrepreneur. Yet both of you agree that the stuff on websites that is 'conventional business guidance' such as 'How to come up with a great business idea?', 'How to pitch your idea to investors?', 'Getting finance' 'There's a business in you', 'What needs to be in your business plan?', 'Get a mentor from a Bank or Corporate', 'Business is Great' and 'How to sell' won't help you to successfully start your business. Why? Because it isn't in the real world of now – much of it is 'old hat' and, thankfully, ignored by anyone under 25.

The enterprise essentials are much less complicated and far more common sense and natural than this guidance.

Most successful entrepreneurs that I've interviewed haven't done any of the things that are regarded as 'good business practice'. Most don't like borrowing money, especially from banks. Their business planning is always in their head. Most of them are action rather than words people. They often copy and improve other people's ideas and activities like crazy. The point is that time is money and opportunities come and go and they can't be wasting time on this theoretical business stuff.

Instead, my advice to a start-up, from my award winning series of entrepreneur interviews (see my book 'Freedom from Bosses Forever') is look for what customers want and are buying that you'd relish providing too.

Then, preferably by bootstrapping, check that you can afford to produce it as a product or service. Then test market your product or service with its 'twist', like Louboutin's red sole or, more likely, with an additional service that the competition aren't providing.

Then from what you have learned launch your new business always remembering that you may need more products and services or even businesses to make the earnings you need to make.

This 'copying and improving with a twist' is important to the success of many entrepreneurs.

For example, the unique 'twist' that Stefan Topfer achieves with WinWeb is that he is absolutely passionate about beating the global competition not just by great cloud software and infrastructure but with data integration through all their services added to exceptional customer service. His customer service people are mentors. He'll sack people that 'sell' his products and services as he believes in the customer buying what they choose that is absolutely right for them.

The great news is that everyone starting a business on their own can provide their own 'twist', a unique level of service, to support a product or service that customers already understand, want and need. Just get your offer out there as quickly as you can after testing

Check it out and go – planning and processes are for the corporates. This is enterprise – get it? That is the point and my final tip:

TIP 20: NEVER GET CONNED INTO BELIEVING THE PLAN WITH THE 'BIG NEW BUSINESS IDEA' IS WHAT YOU NEED. WHAT YOU NEED TO BUILD YOUR BUSINESS ARE PRODUCTS AND SERVICES, WHICH YOU'VE TESTED, THAT PEOPLE WILL WANT TO BUY FROM YOU

__ Finis __

What they've said about Freedom from Bosses Forever:

For your interest, here are some reader reviews of the original version of this book which was entitled 'Stripping for Freedom'.

Reader reviews of 'Freedom from Bosses Forever' can be found on Amazon and this book has a 5 star customer rating. Book critics' reviews can be found on the 'Freedom from Bosses Forever' Facebook page and at http://TonyRobinsonOBE.com and http://FreedomfromBossesForever.com

***

'I've discovered a rare treat. A business book that's valuable and very funny too.'

By Dave Sumner-Smith who is former editor/programme director of b2b business hub, Home Business Network and Telegraph Business Club

When is the last time you read a business book that made you laugh out loud? Every month there seems to be scores of new books about different aspects of business. But many of them seem to cover the same old ground. Very few focus on the special issues relating to running a business from home. And very, very few have ever made me laugh.

'Stripping for Freedom' is an exception to the rule. Written by the Canadian 'writer, broadcaster and celebrity' Leonora Soculitherz (no, I hadn't heard of her either), the book revolves around the basic principle that your business should be based on offering whatever you have got that is wanted by people with money. Even if that means you end up as a lap dancer (though doing that at home is unlikely to generate much revenue, I suspect!).

Written in a fun, bold style that you will either love or hate, it is peppered with 'Leonorisms' ("Leave your old company style behind you. You are now your own brand, so dress to impress") and other advice. When talking about 'Dealing with Regulations', for example, she advises that you should "be generally aware of the regulations around your own enterprise, but don't fall into the trap of trying to comply with it all. Comply only when you have to. Get this wrong and you'll find you're legal but bust, because you had no time or money left to start and run your business."

'Can I sue for emotional stress?!'

By Eva Davies who is Owner/Director, The Electric Zone Online retailer selling luxury electronics, intelligent gadgets and contemporary furniture

OK Tony I am most displeased with you and Clare – you shouldn't have written such a funny book.

Picture the scene – we are taking a family holiday in Brighton and I have found a good deal at The Grand Hotel (swanky or what)

One afternoon it is raining so I decide to have tea and a nice read in the lounge. I stupidly took Stripping for Freedom with me and firstly had raised eyebrows from the waiter. Secondly and worst – I started laughing aloud so hard that it came out as a snort – v. embarrassing – other guests lowered their copies of the Telegraph and Wisden to look disapprovingly at me!

Seriously it is so funny, Tony.

Do hope I get to meet you in the flesh in the future. Do you venture south – Londoners are quite friendly once you get over the language barrier

Have got to go and cut down my thick tights now – thank Leonora for the tip – us good Indian girls don' t like to waste money!

'The funniest hard-hitting business book, that is absolutely full of business truth'

By Stefan Topfer who is Chairman and CEO WinWeb Global entrepreneur, cloud software and apps and Editor of The Small Business Blog

"Soculitherz has written books before, but this one is, in my opinion, the best she has ever written for anyone who wants to take control of their own destiny by going it alone. At the same time this is the funniest hard-hitting business book, that is absolutely full of business truth, I have ever read – some have called this book "whacky" and I can agree with that to some extent. Why else would I now deny to sitting her in winter at my home desk with my fleece on – heck, I even would deny owning a fleece.

Confused? Fasten your seat belt and read the book and find out why Zsa Zsa Gabor, "...wanted a man who only has to be kind and understanding. Is that too much to ask of a multi-millionaire?" Find out why this book is not only for women and why it is so relevant for you and your entrepreneurial endeavours.

Leonora, with the help of her "underwhelming" helper Tony Robinson, cuts through the chase, tells it how it is and then delivers the distilled business truth in a fashion that entertains as much as it is relevant.

"Stripping" for freedom paints a picture of brutally honest business acumen and asks you how much you really want it – and by getting you to strip your ambitions bare in the process of reading, this book leaves you in no doubt on who has to make it happen – You!

If you plan to read one book this holiday season, make it "Stripping for Freedom" – you will by mightily entertained with humorous insights, exposed yet practical business knowledge whilst being delighted and amused with the double meaning of words. I guess as you can tell, I loved this book,.... just don't tell her about the fleece – you must promise!"

'Well worth absorbing'

By Gail Purvies a writer who edits Compute Scotland in which this review appeared. Gail was also a friend from school days of the late Miles Kington, the brilliant humorous writer.

Ably assisted by Tony Robinson (who despite this, emerges as the fall guy) and judiciously edited by Clare Francis, author Leonora Soculitherz, takes her own ultra fashionably, chatty, confidential route through "Stripping for Freedom" or "taking control of your own destiny by going it alone" as an entrepreneur.

For lazy readers with an urge to get at the key issues, nothing is easier than page flicking for Leonorisms or 'truths" helpfully printed in easily seen bold lettering. The first one is core to the whole book. 'Think of a lap dancer: what have you got to offer that people with money to spend, want?'

Closely followed by "in a recession, don't just fish in the private sector pool for your customers because the public sector fish are fatter and easier to catch (especially between January to the end of March when they have got to get rid of all that's remaining of their budgets and allowances).

For a Scottish biased website, it's a pleasure to see good work being recognised. Leonora points out 'The Highlands and Islands of Scotland recognise the importance of providing consistently high levels of free training and support to start up and existing micro enterprise owners to ensure they have the same chance of success as in any other career.'

On essential effective networking the highlight is 'choose productive networks from which you can learn, gain a profile and be given and give referrals.'

But this idle approach will lose the humour, and some interesting and reflective stories, well worth absorbing. Take the chapter on Scarborough. Why Scarborough? Well it's hats off to Scarborough, which with a population of 50,000 first won "The Most Enterprising Place in Yorkshire,' then 'The Most Enterprising place in Britain,' to be ultimately crowned in Prague as, 'The Most Enterprising Town in Europe.' That Scarborough chapter has lots to teach any budding business owner.

The best Leonorism is of course the last, and concerns the daily topping up of the three pots. But you've got 183 pages to strip through first, by which time you should have worked out the three pot issue.

'Laughing Out Loud'

By Julie Stanford who is a designer, radio presenter and President of Brighton & Hove Chamber of Commerce. Julie developed, owns and publishes through Cobweb, the Essential Business Guide - the top UK reference guide for small business owners.

I'm really enjoying reading Stripping for Freedom' (indeed my snort of laughter woke up a few sleeping travellers on a Brighton to Victoria train when I read the part about looking good being simply a matter of how well you tuck in your bits!)

'An Essential Read'

By Dr Robert Murray who was formerly Enterprise Coordinator at Nottingham Trent University

Being retired, I read this book just for its humour. It certainly succeeded in that respect as the jokes and situations were to my liking. However, the important messages came across and I have spent the weeks since I read Leonora's thesis, telling my friends that the country is simply doing the wrong things.

Why do we spend tens of thousands of pounds to create one job in the big, high tech, industries when a few hundred would give the small entrepreneur the time to become established? Why don't we support small business and encourage the ideas that come from people of all ages?

Fantastic advice in the book and it does mean freedom to liberate people to accomplish a successful business that is their dream.

We need Leonora in a position of power to save us from the professional, blinkered politicians, particularly those who are in power from their titles rather than from the ballot box.

'Light style, serious message'

By George Derbyshire OBE who was Chief Executive of the National Federation of Enterprise Agencies

Books about entrepreneurship come in different styles, but usually all end up as lists. This one is different. Persevere: amidst the anecdotes and the quirky humour there is lots of serious guidance for new entrepreneurs. And some questions which ought to make one or two people in Whitehall shuffle on their seats in embarrassment. Why does nearly all the government money go to the usual suspects?

'Entertaining and informative'

By Anthony Haynes who is a Literary Agent, Publisher and Co-Owner of Higher & Professional

The framework of this book is a narrative told by a Canadian author (and style guru) exploring entrepreneurship (and the lack of support for micro-enterprises) in the UK. The structure makes the book both entertaining (I particularly liked the portrait of Jools, the businesswoman who ruins everyone's train journey by yelling into her mobile throughout the journey) and informative: there's good, down to earth, advice for people running, or intending to run, their own (genuinely) small businesses. And there are some good jokes too.

'Fancy a Leonorism...?'

By Nat Hardwick who is a Musician, IT Consultant and Director of the UK Sector Skills Body for Small Firms and Business Support – SFEDI Group

What a thoroughly enjoyable read...! By turns satirical, thought-provoking and darkly comic. Many a laugh-out-loud moment... Leonora takes us on a whistle stop tour de force of our own entrepreneurial culture and holds up a (wildly fashionable) mirror... but don't be surprised if you don't like all that you see!

Contact Details

Tony Robinson OBE Speaker & Author

http://TonyRobinsonOBE.com

http://FreedomfromBossesForever.com

http://MicroBizMattersDay.rocks

Twitter: @TonyRobinsonOBE and on LinkedIn & Facebook & Pinterest & YouTube

E-mail: TonyRobinsonOBE@gmail.com

Enterprise Rockers Free & Indie, Global Community of micro business owners.

http://EnterpriseRockers.co.uk

http://EnterpriseRockers.com

http://MicroBizMattersDay.rocks

Twitter: @EnterpriseRocks & #MicroBizMattersDay

and Groups on LinkedIn & Facebook

Cover Design by LoveYourCovers.com

Formatted by JoHarrison.rocks

ABOUT THE AUTHORS

Soculitherz is a Canadian fashionista, investigative journalist and author of this, 'the funniest book on enterprise'. Soculitherz is also a Global Ambassador for the Enterprise Rockers Community. This is free to join, once you have started your business, and makes life better for micro-enterprises everywhere. See EnterpriseRockers.co.uk

Leonora Soculitherz was born in Ottawa and graduated in English and Canadian Literature from Toronto University. In 1990 she married the famous English cellist and composer Gerard Brown and settled in London. Her first book, published in 1991, was a manual for self discovery and fulfilment called 'Enhancing Life in Lemon or Peach'. This had sufficient success for Leonora to begin weekly columns on fashion, self fulfilment and nutrition in a number of journals and magazines.

Separated from Gerard Brown, after a well publicised and televised incident during Elgar's Cello Concerto in 1992, Leonora moved to Corfu. It was in Corfu that she wrote her best selling and Kanawa International Book prize winning first novel, 'The Edible Desire'. This was hailed as a classic of 'magical realism' and was quickly followed up by 'Bong in the Orange Grove', which was made into the film 'Sweet Oranges, Bitter Lemons'.

In the early noughties, seeming to tire of the book and film promotion circuit, Leonora was heard more on radio, back in England once again. She hosted her own popular, weekly Country and Cajun Music show and also did special interviews of famous personalities from the worlds of show business, politics, sports and business, particularly on the causes of their 'inner drive'. She continued to write for the quality press and published her autobiography 'Over Strung and Under Nourished' at the end of 2002.

In 2004 the mythical Soculitherz worked for the first time with Tony Robinson OBE to write her first book on best business practice entitled 'Buzzing with the Entrepreneurs'. She called the experience 'unforgettable' and has been seen infrequently in the UK since. In 2009, enticed by a large advance, she agreed to collaborate with Robinson, for a maximum of forty days. The result was 'Stripping for Freedom'. 'Stripping' was updated and improved by Tony Robinson OBE, in 2013/14, to become 'Freedom from Bosses Forever' much to the disgust of Soculitherz.

Tony Robinson OBE co-founded, the free-to-join-in, Enterprise Rockers Community Interest company, with the fabulous Tina Boden, in January 2012. Enterprise Rockers is a global self help community making business life better for micro (0-9 employees) business owners. Tony writes and speaks on enterprise and is one third of the '#MicroBizMatters Show' which helps employees of large companies and the public sector provide higher levels of customer service to business owners.

You can follow Tony at http://TonyRobinsonOBE.com and http://EnterpriseRockers.co.uk and http://MicroBizMattersDay.rocks

On Twitter he is @TonyRobinsonOBE and @EnterpriseRocks and #MicroBizMattersDay

He is also on LinkedIn, Facebook, Google+, Pinterest and YouTube as Tony Robinson OBE

Since 1986 his other enterprise, which he founded with his best friend, Clare Francis, BAB the Business Advisory Bureau Limited, allows him to guide and coach individuals who want to go it alone as independent professionals. Many are executives facing redundancy or just desperate to cut the chains of the corporate cubicle. They, or their employer, choose to pay BAB as a high quality, private sector alternative to government funded start up support.

Tony is regarded by his peers as one of the UK's leading experts on enterprise - promotion, engagement, policy, skills and development. He was honoured to receive from Prince Charles at Buckingham Palace, in 2001, an OBE for services to small firms and training. In 2012 he received from the IAB, at the House of Commons, a Lifetime Achievement Award for Enterprise. In December 2013, Start Your Business Magazine, gave him a Lifetime Achievement Award for his contribution to enterprise support.

He tries to bring humour into all his speaking engagements and writing on the micro enterprise revolution throughout the world and has researched the essential skills to succeed in your own enterprise. He has spoken at over 140 enterprise and entrepreneurship conferences in the UK and overseas. He is the author of seven books of which Freedom from Bosses Forever is his 'pride and joy'. He writes blogs and articles on enterprise for many global publications including http://sme-blog.com and http://businesszone.co.uk.

www.ingramcontent.com/pod-product-compliance
Lightning Source LLC
Chambersburg PA
CBHW071026080526
44587CB00015B/2511